Get OUT there!

A colouring book to inspire new adventures

igloobooks

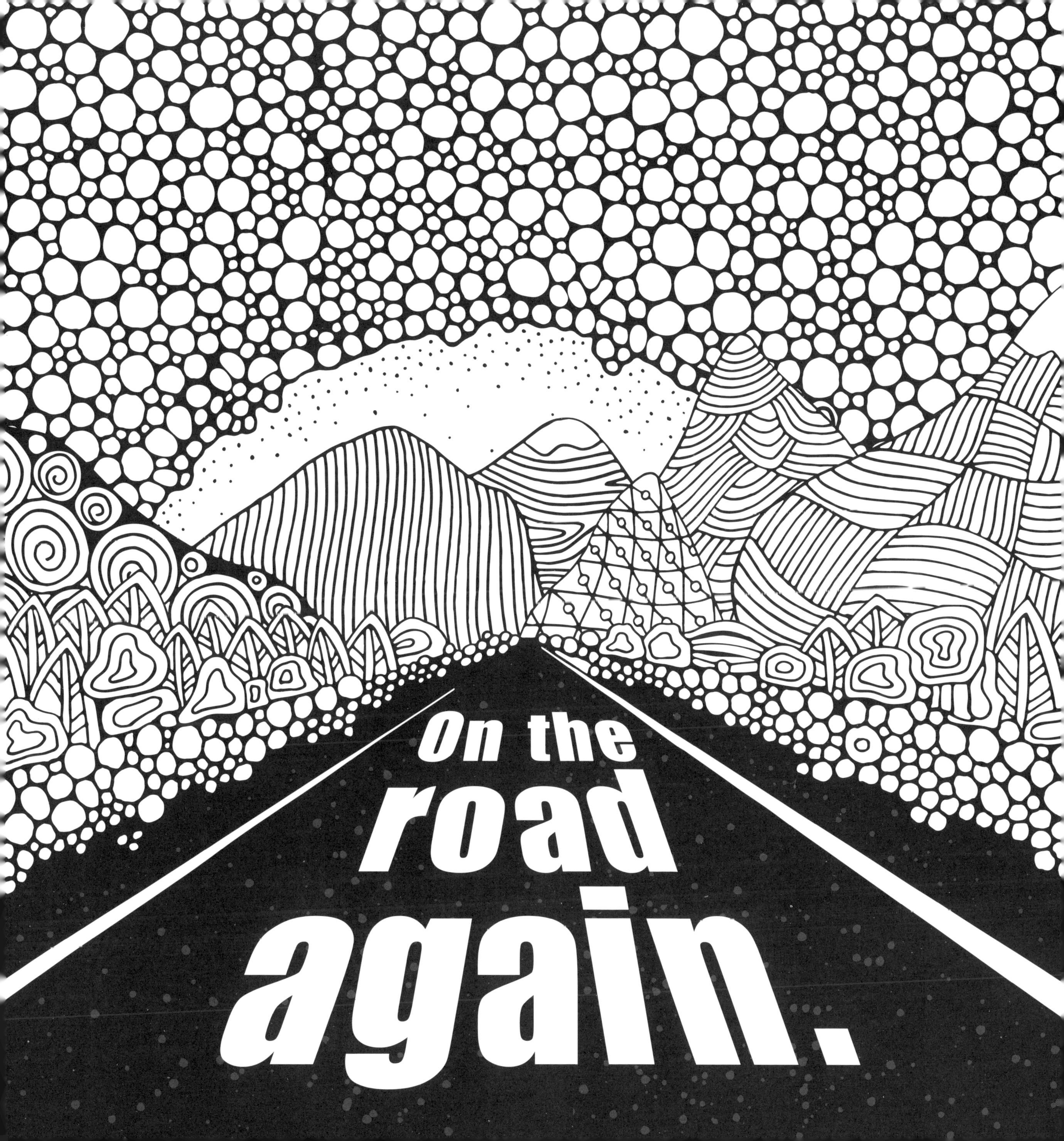
On the
road
again.

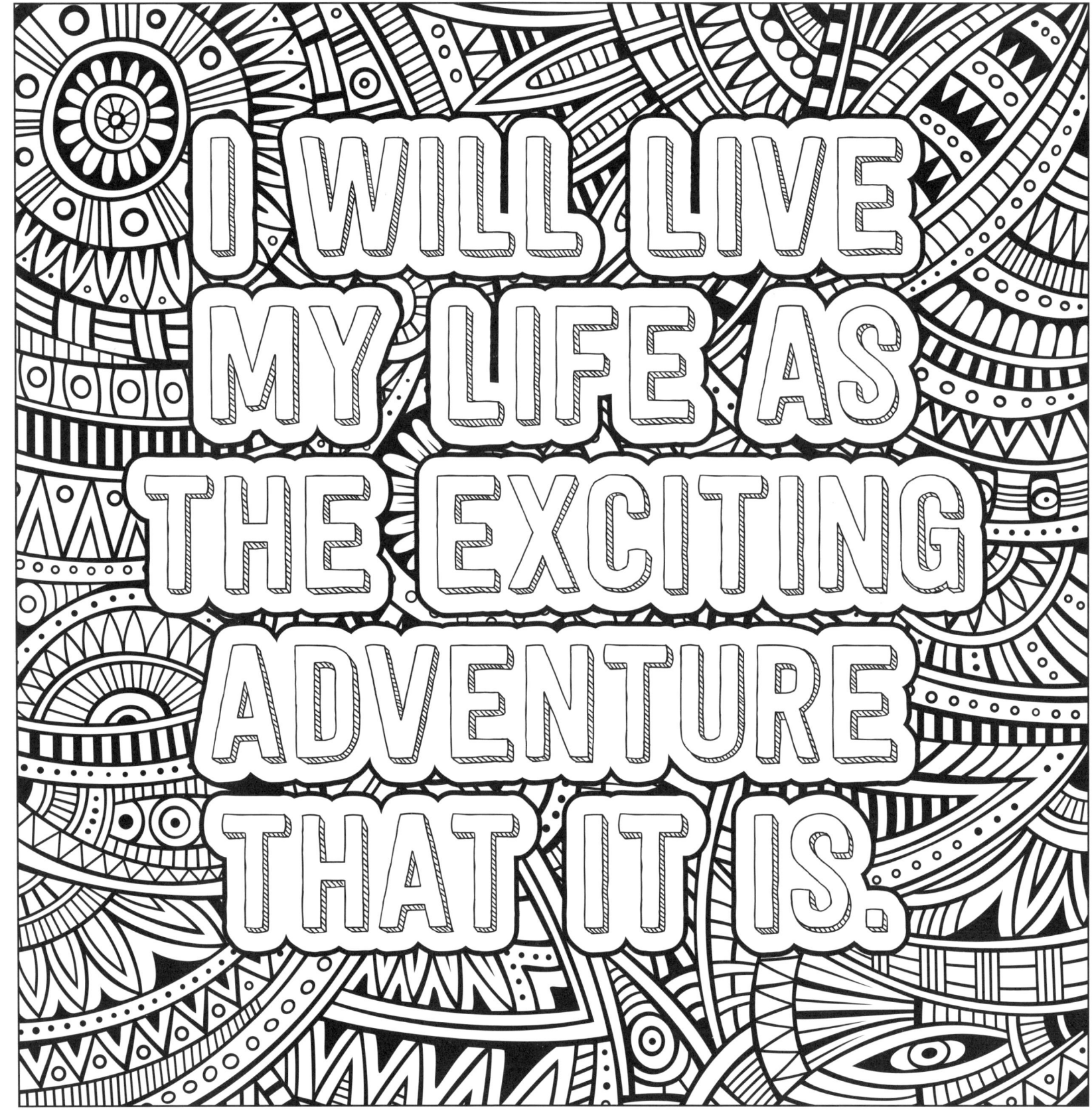

THE JOURNEY IS JUST AS

IMPORTANT AS THE DESTINATION.

Wherever I am

is where I need to be.

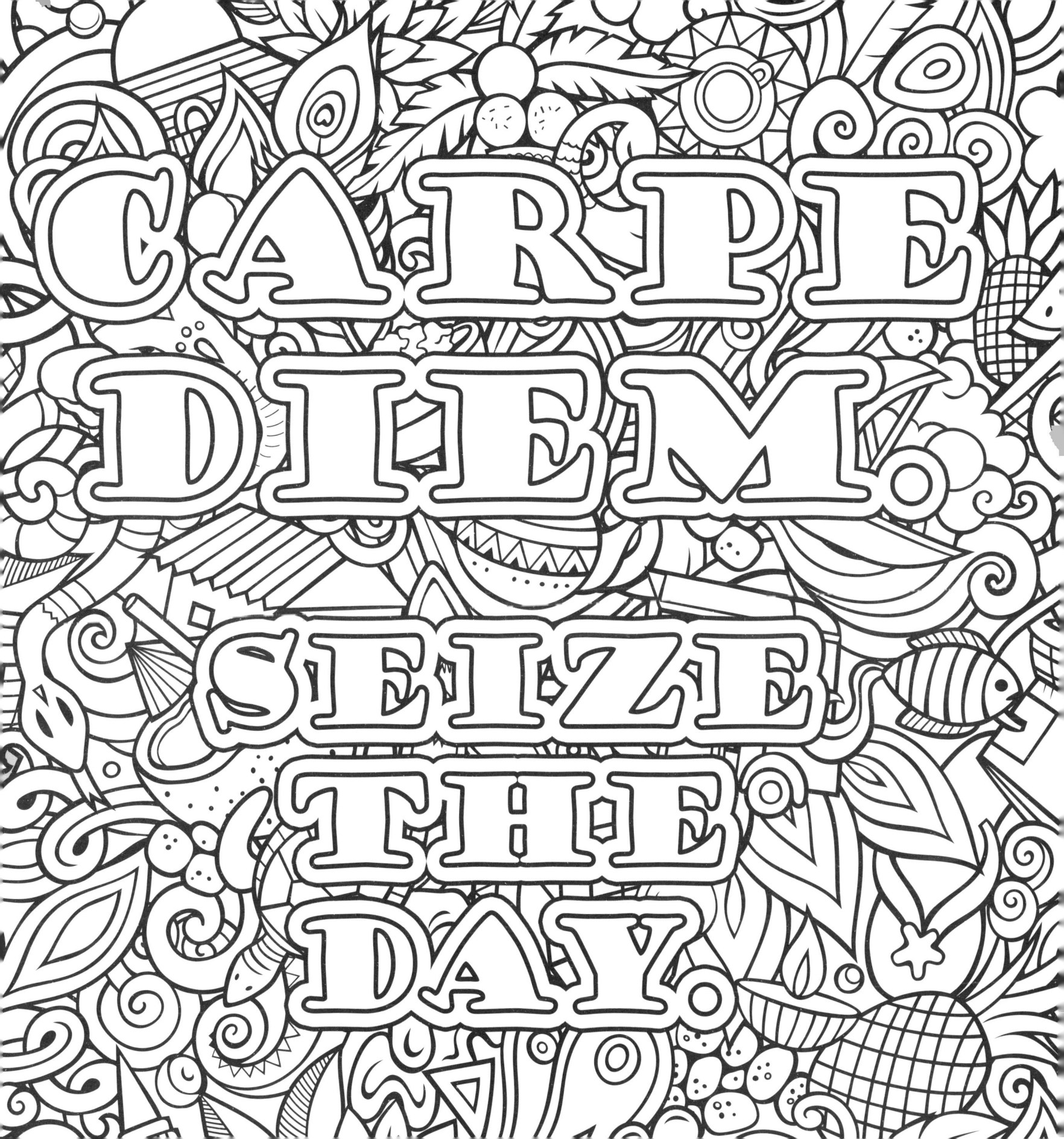

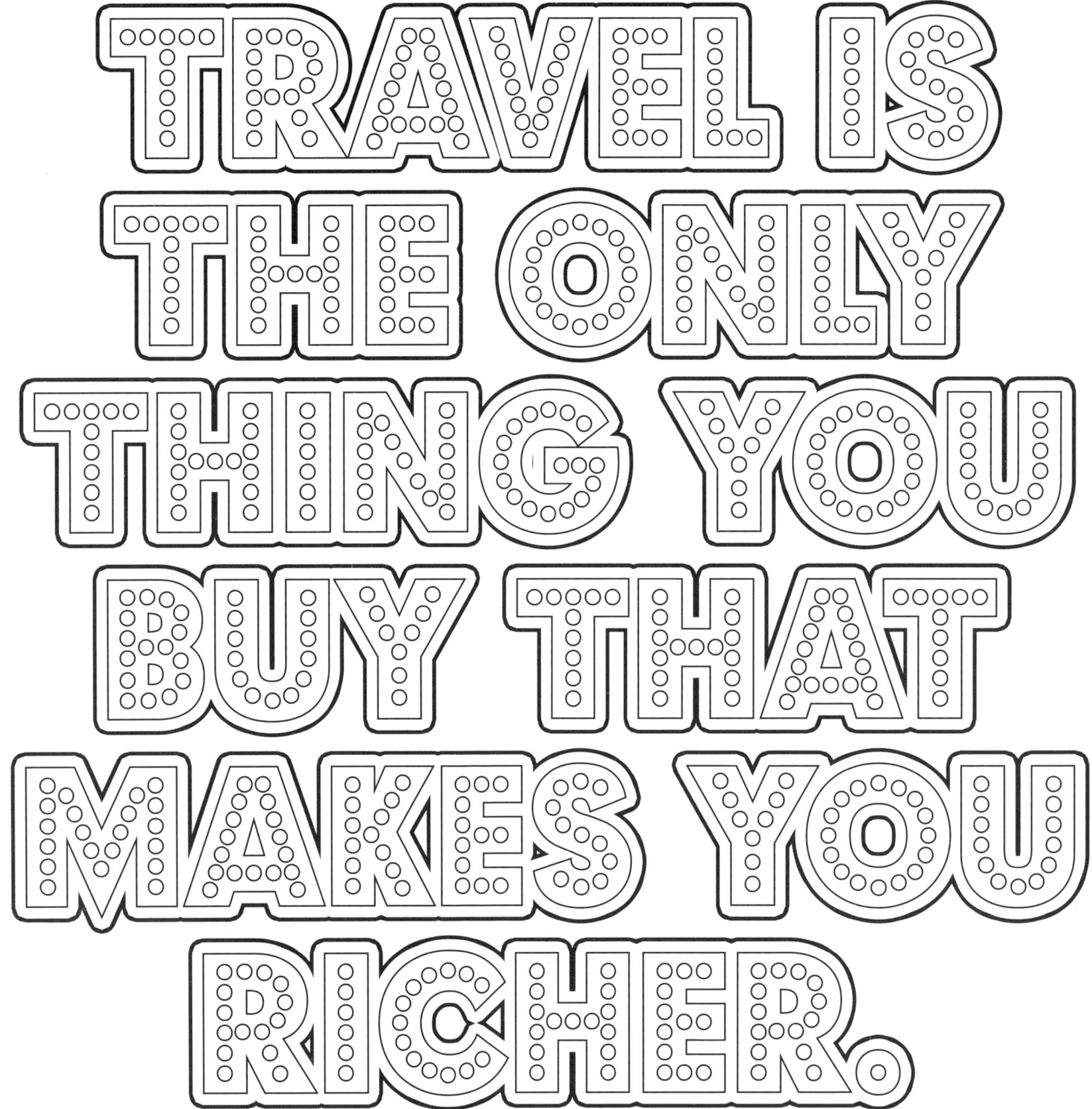

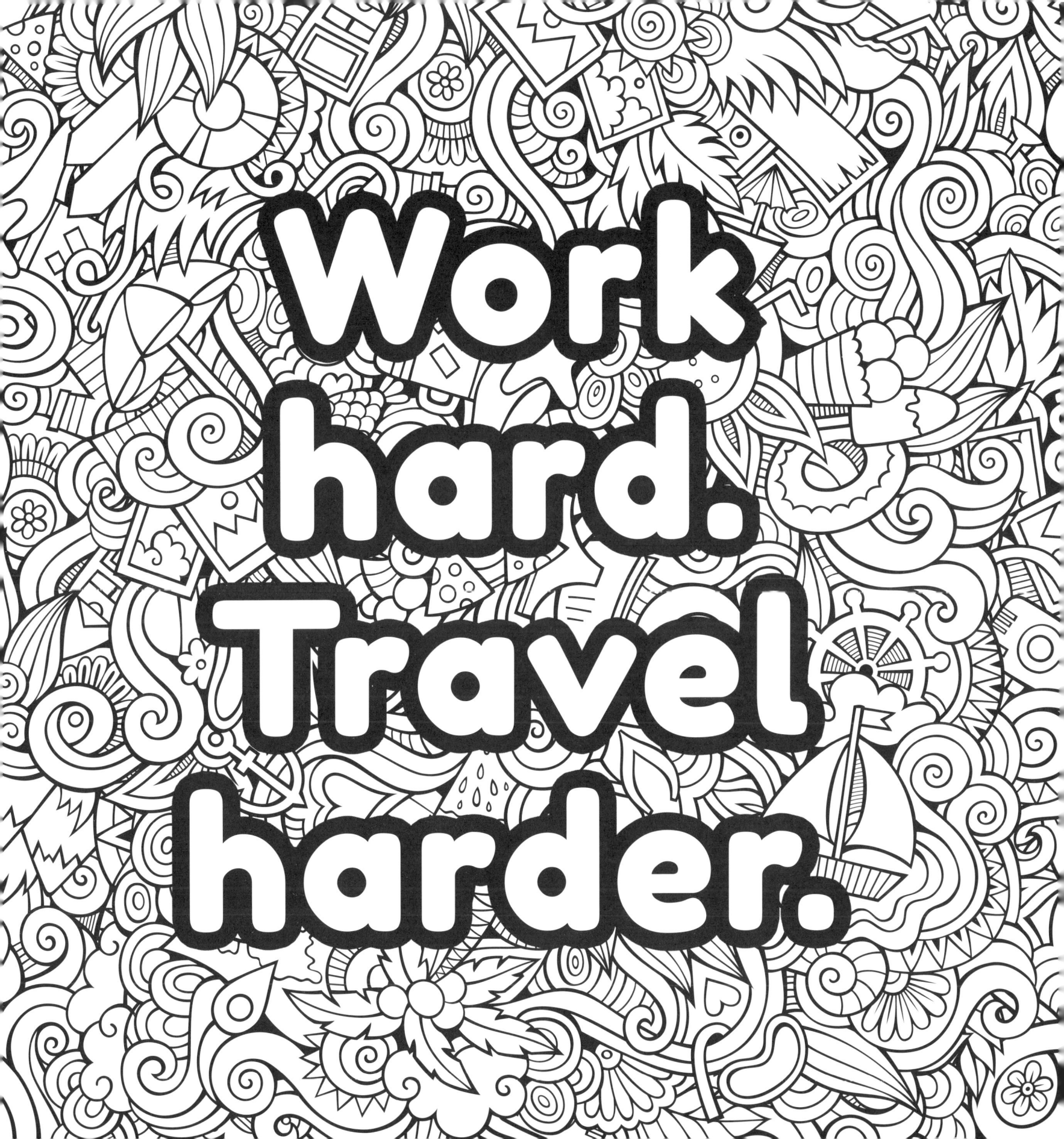

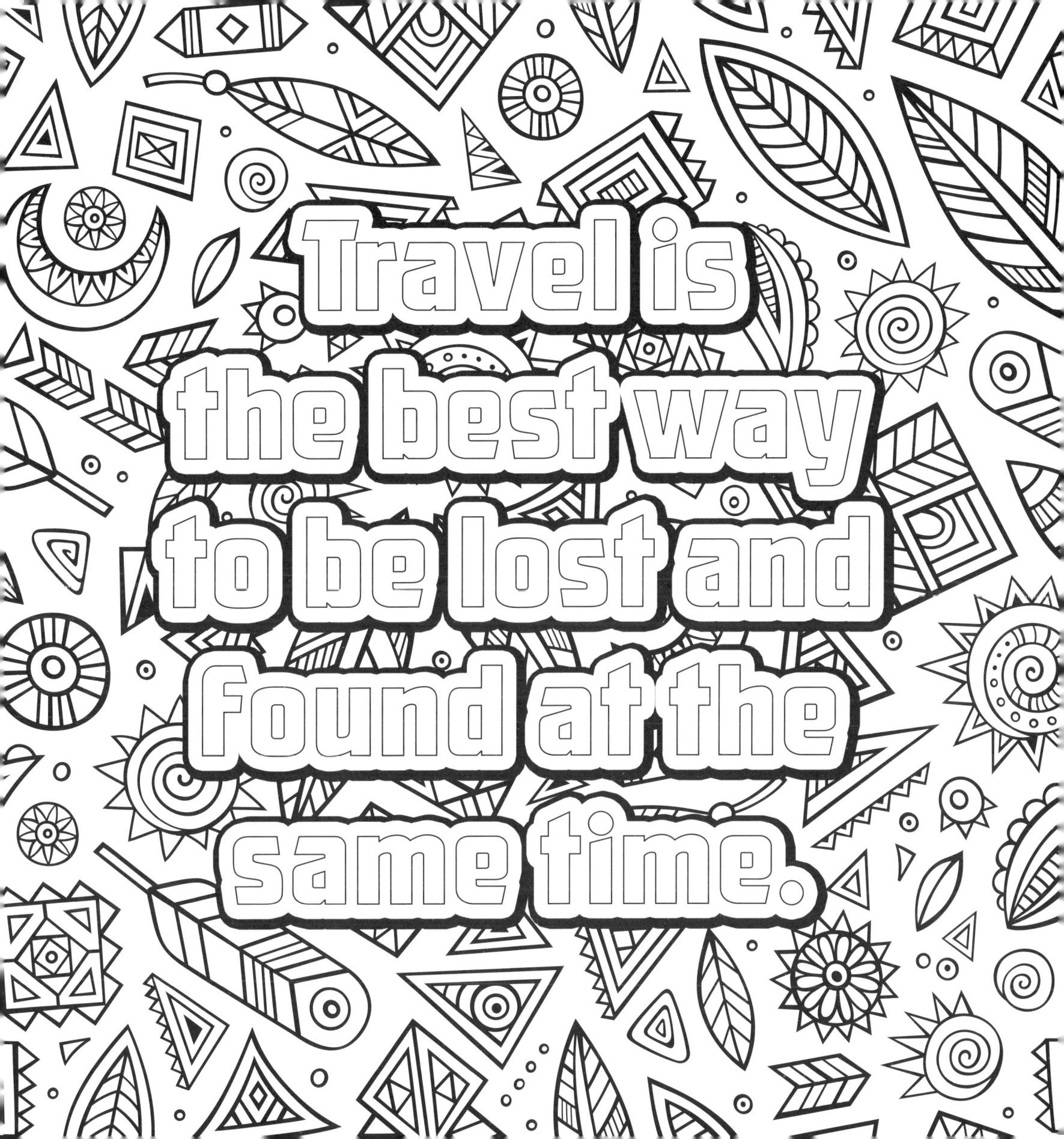

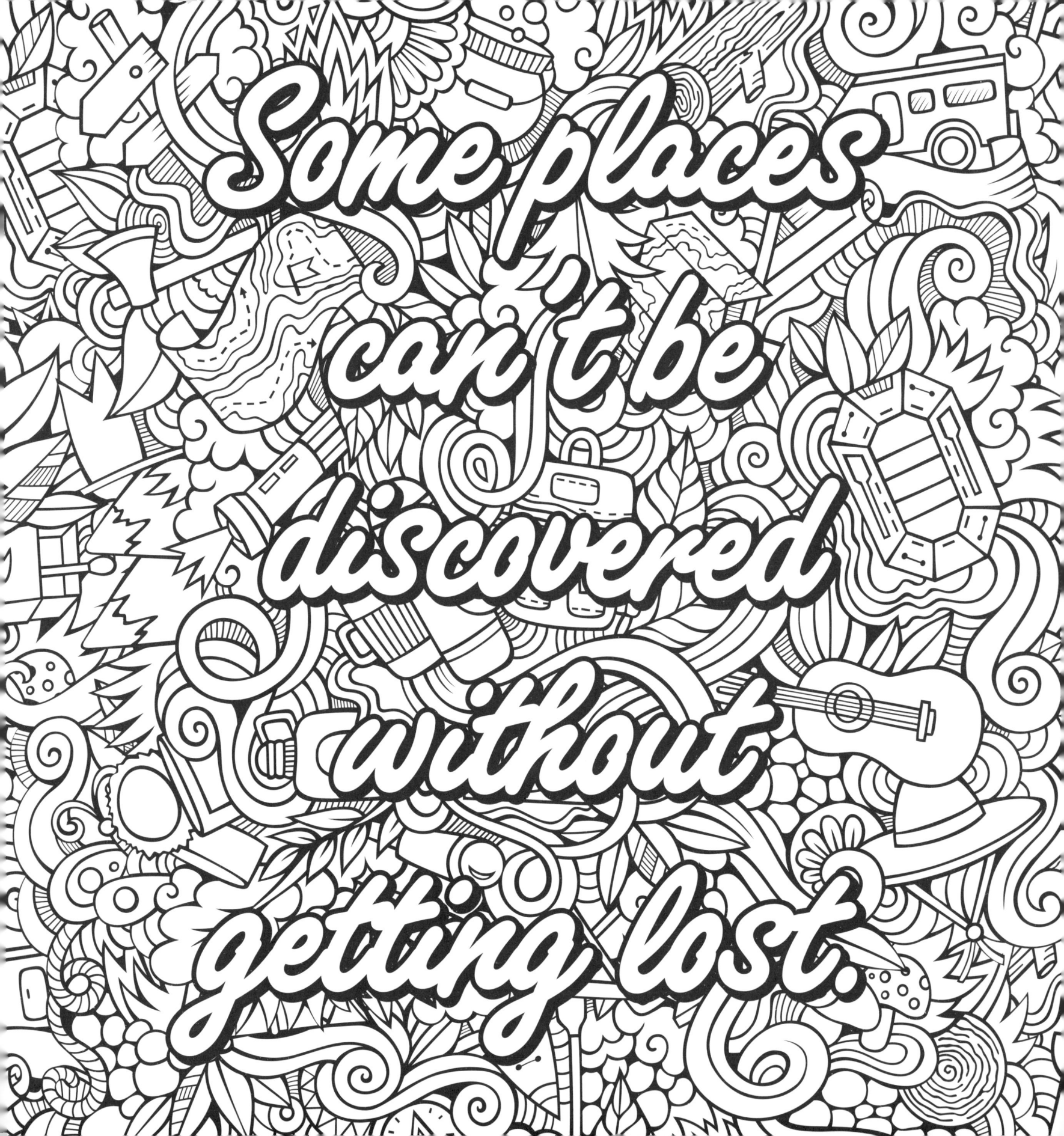

The more I travel, the closer I get to a life full of adventure.

I'll keep me safe, adventure can keep me wild.